DITCH THE GIT.....BEFORE IT'S TOO LATE

DITCH THE GIT.....BEFORE IT'S TOO LATE

JACK MALLORY

Every Cloud

CONTENTS

I dedicate this book to all of you out there who deserve a life of love and happiness. Don't settle for second best. Your soul mate is out there, you just need to look.

CHAPTER 1

The Facts

I may not possess the academic credentials or formal training in the fields of love and relationships that some experts boast about. I don't have degrees or doctorates hanging on my wall, and I haven't spent years in classrooms or research labs studying these topics. However, what I do have is something I consider far more precious and insightful: real-life experience. Unlike those who pursued these subjects perhaps as a default career choice or out of lack of better options, I have lived through the highs and lows, the joys and heartbreaks of relationships. This hands-on experience has taught me lessons that no textbook or lecture ever could. So, while I may not be a traditional 'expert,' my insights come from the school of hard knocks, and I believe they can be incredibly valuable to you.

Let me introduce you to a concept you may or may not be familiar with: 'falling in love with love itself.' This phrase describes a common trap where people become enamoured with the idea or fantasy of being in love rather than truly understanding or connecting with the person they're with. It's about romanticizing the notion of love and the experiences it brings—flowers, dates, declarations of affection—without considering the deeper, sometimes more challenging realities of a relationship. If this idea is new to you, don't worry. I'm here to guide you through understanding it because recognizing this pitfall can be crucial in avoiding a future filled with unhappiness and regret. Stick with me, and together we'll navigate through this complex terrain.

The essence of this book is captured perfectly in its title: 'ditch the git before it is too late.' The message is straightforward: you need to be fully aware of who your potential partner is, including all their good and bad traits. Relationships should be approached with a discerning eye, not a blind heart. If you find that the negative aspects of your partner far outweigh the positive ones, it's crucial to end the relationship before its too late and they end up causing you more harm than good. For those unfamiliar with the term, a 'git' is a British slang term akin to calling someone an 'asshole.' It's a less harsh, yet still pointed, way to describe someone who might not be good for you. I considered using stronger language for the title but opted for something that would be relatable and accessible to all genders. With that explanation out of the way, let's dive into the heart of the matter and start this journey together.

The dream of experiencing a fairytale love affair and true happiness is something that resonates deeply within all of us. Since childhood, I've always envisioned finding a woman whom I could love wholeheartedly and who would reciprocate that love with equal fervour. I'm here to tell you that such a love truly exists. It's not just a figment of our collective imagination. For me, however, the journey to find it was far from straightforward—it took forty-two years and two failed marriages. Yet, when I finally found my true partner, I experienced a level of happiness and contentment I had never known before. My wife is beautiful, caring, loving, and unselfish. She loves me for who I am, not for who she thinks she can mold me into. This genuine love is mutual, and I am as happy as a pig in... well, let's just say I've never been happier.

I'll never forget the sight of tears streaming down the cheeks of my wonderful eleven-year-old son when his mother and I told him we were getting divorced. That moment is etched in my memory forever. It's a pain I wouldn't wish on anyone, and the ripple effects of that moment have influenced my life in countless ways. This profound experience, along with the subsequent challenges and realizations, motivated me to write this book. Initially, I intended it to be a guide on what to avoid in a potential partner and how to recognize warning signs. However, as I wrote, it evolved into much more. This book now encompasses a wide array of issues that may arise during a relationship or marriage.

As you read, you might find yourself wondering how one person could endure so many challenges. Trust me, when you compare my experiences with your own and create a mental checklist of similar occurrences, you'll likely be surprised at the parallels. My hope is that by sharing my journey, you'll gain valuable insights and perhaps avoid some of the pitfalls I encountered.

This book is part self-help and part advice, drawn from

my personal experiences. It's meant to be a practical guide to navigating the complexities of relationships, recognizing potential problems, and understanding the dynamics that can make or break a partnership. Whether you're just starting out in love or looking to improve an existing relationship, I believe there's something here for everyone. Let's embark on this journey together and discover how to find and nurture the love we all dream of.

I often hear people joke about needing to ask their partner's permission before they can do something or go somewhere. Unfortunately, beneath the humour lies a troubling reality of controlling or bullying behaviour in some relationships. I remember once discussing a potential new role at work with a male colleague. This role would require me to work on Saturdays. I mentioned that I needed to discuss it with my wife, as she might adjust her work schedule to align with mine. At home, we talked it over, and she mentioned she didn't like the idea of working weekends but said it was ultimately my decision. That conversation solidified my choice; I'd rather spend my weekends with her than at work. When I relayed this to my colleague, his immediate response was, "Wouldn't she let you?"

This reaction is something I hear often, particularly from men, and it always strikes me as a sign that they might feel controlled by their partners. In my relationship, my wife and I deeply value our time together. We work to live, not the other way around. This concept of prioritizing time with loved ones over work seems hard for some to grasp, which is one of the reasons I decided to write this book.

To me, a marriage or relationship should be a loving

partnership where you share life, enjoy mutual interests, and genuinely want to be together. While it's important for each person to have their own hobbies and interests, no one should feel restricted or controlled by their partner. At the same time, these personal interests shouldn't take precedence over the relationship. Love and life are about balance and compromise.

As I've mentioned before, I didn't find my perfect partner until I was 42 years old. The years leading up to that moment were filled with heartache and challenges. My goal in writing this book is to help you avoid similar misery and find genuine happiness in your relationships.

So, dear reader, this book is a candid, no-holds-barred guide for both men and women. I'm not concerned with being politically correct, and I make no apologies for expressing my thoughts bluntly. Prepare yourself for an unfiltered exploration of love and life. Hold on tight—it's going to be a down-to-earth ride on the roller coaster of relationships.

CHAPTER 2

The Attraction

Everyone has a certain level of intuition, which plays a significant role in forming initial impressions when meeting someone new. Within the first thirty seconds of an encounter, our subconscious mind assesses various cues—body language, tone of voice, eye contact—and makes snap judgments about the person's character. This rapid evaluation helps us decide if we feel a connection, whether we want to pursue a friendship, and if we believe we will get along with them. This instinctive ability often improves with age and experience. As a child, I could often sense the presence of a bully or selfish person from a mile away, and this skill has only become more refined as I've grown older.

Despite this intuitive ability, I found myself with two failed marriages. The reason? The old adage, "love is blind," rings true. Love can obscure our judgment, causing us to overlook warning signs and ignore our gut feelings. When we're deeply infatuated, we might see only what we want to see, missing the red flags that would otherwise be obvious. It took me some time and hard lessons, but eventually, I learned to balance love with discernment. When I met my current wife, it was like finding a missing puzzle piece. We are soul mates who genuinely love and appreciate each other's company, making me realize how beautiful life can be when shared with the right person.

Whether we admit it or not, the quest for a life partner underlies much of our dating behaviour. Each time we consider a potential girlfriend or boyfriend, our subconscious mind is at work, checking off attributes that align with our vision of a soul mate. Dating is not just about immediate attraction; it's about evaluating compatibility for a long-term relationship. Some might date with the intention of a fleeting romance or a one-night stand. While there's no judgment here, that's not the focus of this discussion. For those of us seeking meaningful connections, such prospects are quickly filtered out.

To navigate this search effectively, the first step is to understand what attracts you to a potential partner. Is it their physical appearance, body shape, personality, sense of humour, or shared interests? The list of qualities can be endless and unique to each individual. However, it's safe to say that many of us are looking for a soul mate—someone who is attractive both externally and internally. While physical attraction is important, inner beauty and compatibility are what sustain a relationship in the long run. After all, beauty is subjective, and the most important thing is finding someone whose qualities resonate with you deeply.

In essence, love and life are about balance, mutual respect, and shared joy. Relationships thrive on give and take, understanding, and appreciating each other's individuality while building a life together. By recognizing what truly matters to you in a partner and staying true to your values, you can navigate the complexities of love with greater clarity and purpose.

No matter what people might say, the first thing that attracts you to someone is undeniably their outward appearance. It's a natural instinct. Everyone has an image in their mind of their ideal partner. You might be drawn to someone who is slim, large, or athletic. You could prefer someone of your own race or be attracted to specific features, like blue eyes and blonde hair. You won't truly know or be certain until that pivotal moment arrives.

Personally, I never had a concrete image of my ideal partner in my mind. I believed that when you meet the right person, you'll just know. However, as I navigated the rocky road of life, encountering various situations and making mistakes—or having them forced upon me—I gradually developed a clearer picture, even a checklist, of what I desired in a life partner.

Before joining the Army at the age of 19, I led a sheltered life. My strict upbringing meant I was neither allowed nor encouraged to have a girlfriend. Joining the Army exposed me to a diverse range of individuals, both men and women, who were far more experienced in the ways of the world and the dating scene. As a fresh-faced young lad, I found myself among people who not only had experience with romantic relationships but also openly boasted about their conquests. This environment was a stark contrast to my sheltered past and served as an eye-opener to the realities of the world. Despite the boasting and bravado, I always believed that such matters were personal. To this day, I've never discussed my love life with anyone—except my wife, of course.

In your mind, you might have a picture or a list of qualities you're looking for in a partner. It's common to meet potential partners at work or school, where you already have a sense of their character. The initial date often confirms or dispels your impression of them, which is crucial. If, during the date, something feels off, it's important to trust your instincts and reconsider the relationship.

A personal example involves meeting the woman who became my first wife. We met at work, and she initially seemed very nice and chatty. However, this was a facade. When I asked her out, she told me she had a boyfriend, so I respectfully backed off. Two weeks later, she suggested we meet up as friends for a day of shopping. When I inquired about her boyfriend, she mentioned they had broken up. Lucky me, I thought.

The first warning sign was how easily she broke off her long-term relationship. Much later, I discovered they had actually been engaged. By then, it was too late—I was already caught in the trap. In hindsight, I should have sensed something was wrong and ended things then and there. Another red flag was her sudden interest in me after seeing my new car and making comments about my perceived wealth. These should have been clear indicators of her true intentions.

The first date or initial meeting is your chance to get to know the other person. While I pride myself on being a good judge of character in work or social situations, I realized that my judgment in matters of the heart was not as sharp. Love, indeed, can be blinding.

In conclusion, navigating the complexities of love and relationships requires a balance of intuition, experience, and self-awareness. Physical attraction might draw us in, but it's the deeper qualities that sustain a relationship. By learning from our experiences and recognizing red flags early on, we can make better choices and find partners who truly complement us. Love might be blind at times, but with the right approach, we can find the clarity we need to build lasting, fulfilling relationships.

CHAPTER 3

The First Date

The first date marks the pivotal beginning of any potential relationship. It's the moment where the foundation of your future together is laid. Beyond the initial spark of attraction, engaging in conversation during that first encounter feels almost like conducting an interrogation. You're seeking to unravel the layers of their personality, learning about their family background, occupation, interests, and dislikes. It's a natural part of the process, essential for understanding if this person aligns with your vision of an ideal partner.

With a clear understanding of your own identity and desires, you embark on a quest to find someone who not only matches your physical and mental ideal but also shares at least some of your interests. It's no easy feat, but it's a journey worth undertaking.

Earlier, I mentioned my lack of a defined criteria for a potential partner. However, I knew I sought kindness, a sense of humour, and perhaps a shared taste in music as a starting point.

Many relationships begin in various settings—a bar, café, restaurant, workplace, or even at a friend's gathering. However, where that initial encounter occurs can significantly influence the trajectory of the relationship. Meeting someone while engaging in an activity you both enjoy; be it an adventurous outing, a sports event, or a hobby,sets a positive tone. Shared interests create a strong foundation from the outset.

Let's delve into the scenario of a first date at a restaurant. While dining out has become more casual in recent times, how your date dresses and presents themselves still holds considerable importance. Their appearance often serves as a significant factor in determining your level of attraction. What you seek in a partner varies greatly based on your own preferences and values. You may gravitate towards someone with a similar adventurous spirit and love for revelry, or perhaps you're in search of a calm, steady presence in your life. Assuming you're a relaxed, sensible individual with a set of values, you're likely seeking a partner with whom you can share happiness, build a life together, and proudly introduce to your family.

Regardless of what anyone may say, initial attraction often begins with physical appearance, akin to admiring the wrapping of a Christmas or birthday gift before delving into its contents. Naturally, on a first date, one tends to dress smartly, yet conservatively, in the hopes of making a favourable impression. But how does your date fare in the appearance department? Each person has their own preferences, so I'm not here to judge anyone's fashion choices. However, it's essential to ask yourself whether you feel comfortable being seen in public with this person. Whether your date is a tattooed and pierced punk rocker, a woman in a figure-hugging, scantily clad dress, or a conservatively dressed individual, the first impression has been made, and now it's up to you to decide whether it aligns with your ideals.

In reality, we all have our turn-offs when it comes to appearances. Some may find excessive makeup or fake tans off-putting, while others may not mind. Personally, I see past the exterior and feel a sense of regret that such beauty is concealed beneath layers of cosmetic enhancements. Similarly, women who opt for revealing outfits may appeal to some but turn off others. The same can be said for men—some may prefer well-dressed gentlemen, while others may be drawn to muscular men sporting sleeveless shirts. Comfort also plays a significant role; if your date's attire doesn't resonate with you, it can create a sense of unease. Moreover, if their style is unusual or outlandish, it might make you feel embarrassed in social settings or when introducing them to your family. Despite this, ultimately, the decision lies with you, guided by your subconscious understanding of what and who you're seeking in a partner.

Once introductions and greetings are out of the way, you may reflect on the encounter. Did you opt for a handshake, a semi-distant wave, or a quick kiss on the cheek? Regardless of the choice, you're now either feeling content or perhaps questioning your actions. Dwelling on it won't change what's already happened, so it's best to move forward with confidence. A firm handshake strikes the right balance at this stage, projecting confidence and setting a positive tone for the rest of the date.

As mentioned earlier, our goal here is to engage in a meaningful conversation with our date, so let's dive in.

Now, who initiates the conversation? Traditionally, it's considered chivalrous to let the lady start, but in modern times, some may view this as sexist. Personally, I find it a courteous gesture that adds warmth to the interaction. However, if you find yourself labelled as sexist when you're simply being polite, it might be wise to reconsider the company you're keeping. After all, if such behaviour persists, it's unlikely to bode well for the future.

Now, on to the conversation itself. What topics should you cover? If you're meeting someone for the first time, this is your chance to get to know them and vice versa. Don't hesitate to ask questions—humans are naturally curious beings and understanding each other's stories is essential for building rapport. Conversation topics can range from basic personal details like age, birthplace, and residence to more personal aspects such as family, career, hobbies, and favourite music. At this stage, you're gaining insights into their life, and with each revelation, you're forming a clearer picture and making mental notes.

Reflecting on my own experiences, when asked to describe myself, I provided a brief and honest overview, highlighting aspects that are important to both myself and a potential partner. Here's an example:

"Hi, I'm XXX, X years old, working as a XXX. I consider myself a happy-go-lucky person, loyal, and affectionate once you get to know me. I'm not the best at ball sports, but I excel in athletics, having participated in several marathons. My musical tastes span various genres, but I have a soft spot for 50s and 60s classics. I'm also passionate about history and proficient in managing finances."

This snippet, though concise, conveys essential aspects of my personality and interests. While it may not resonate with everyone, that's perfectly fine—compatibility is key. Notice how I subtly emphasized the importance of financial responsibility? Based on past experiences, this is a trait I value highly, and it's worth discussing further.

You can often discern someone's hidden agenda by their willingness to agree with everything you say—a trait commonly referred to as being a "yes man" or "yes woman." For instance, I once encountered a person, let's call her woman number one, who claimed to share my musical tastes in the 50s and 60s. Initially, I took her word for it without delving deeper. However, it became apparent much later that she had no genuine interest in the music of that era, when I discovered that she didn't own one record, knew no songs and had no favourite artists. I mean, come on, everyone has at least one favourite singer or song, right, and if you don't, why lie about it? This highlights the importance of probing further from the outset, maintaining an air of calm curiosity. Ask about their favourite songs, artists, and albums. A lack of genuine responses could signify a lack of compatibility and even dishonesty. In such cases, it's best to trust your instincts and part ways before investing further.

Honesty stands as a cornerstone in any relationship, a non-negotiable trait that forms the bedrock of trust and understanding. It's crucial to scrutinize the narratives your date weaves—are they coherent, plausible, and consistent? For instance, encountering an individual under the age of

20 claiming to possess a degree in Engineering and actively working in the field should raise a red flag. Unless they were a prodigy, it's wise to double-check the arithmetic. Yes, this scenario has unfolded before my eyes, underscoring the deceptive allure of rose-tinted glasses.

Furthermore, observe the balance of conversation—is it dominated by tales of their own exploits, with little regard for your interests or experiences? If so, it may hint at a self-centred disposition that could define the trajectory of your relationship. In such cases, it's prudent to reassess the compatibility and consider parting ways with the individual.

Another consideration arises when confronted with a date whose language is peppered with profanity, oblivious to the discomfort it may cause. While enduring it for the duration of the initial meeting might seem tolerable, it begs the question—will this behaviour persist, or can they mature and adapt? Swearing unchecked not only reflects poorly on social etiquette but also poses potential challenges in future interactions, including family dynamics and public settings.

Moving beyond language, table manners offer another glimpse into a person's character. Eating with one's mouth open or displaying excessive drinking habits can be major turn-offs. Likewise, observing how they handle the bill—do they offer to contribute, even if you decline? This simple gesture can speak volumes about their generosity and consideration. However, beware of individuals who exhibit freeloading tendencies, selecting the most expensive items on the menu and feigning ignorance when the bill arrives. Such behaviour not only tarnishes the dining experience but also signals a lack of respect and reciprocity, warranting a swift departure from the relationship.

Assessing a potential partner's character is paramount during the early stages of dating. Pay close attention to how they interact with others and their demeanour throughout the evening—it can offer valuable insights into their personality and compatibility with you.

Observe whether your date exhibits kindness or spends their time making disparaging remarks about others. Criticism towards strangers' fashion choices or demeanour could be a red flag indicating a lack of empathy and respect. Remember, if they are quick to criticize others, they may not hesitate to do the same to you in the future.

Notice their volume when they speak—is it excessively loud, drawing unwanted attention? A boisterous demeanour or lack of social grace can lead to discomfort, making you wish you could retreat into the safety of solitude. Additionally, pay attention to their treatment of wait staff—rudeness towards service staff reflects poorly on their character and may foreshadow future conflicts.

How do they treat you? Are they complimentary or critical of your choices and appearance? A partner who constantly criticizes you is unlikely to foster a supportive and nurturing relationship. Similarly, watch for signs of controlling behaviour—dictating your drink choices or belittling your preferences is a clear indication of disrespect.

Laughter is often touted as the glue that binds relationships. Can you share a laugh with your date, even at the silliest of jokes? A mutual sense of humour and the ability to find joy in each other's company bodes well for the future. In contrast, a partner who is unable to laugh or seeks to dictate what you find amusing may stifle your happiness in the long run.

Assess their digital behaviour—constantly being glued to their phone, taking selfies, or prioritizing calls over your time together may indicate a lack of presence and investment in the relationship. Your time and attention deserve respect, and excessive phone use during dates signals a lack of prioritization.

Finally, take note of shared interests and compatibility—do they appreciate your passions and interests, or do they dismiss them? Mutual respect for each other's hobbies and preferences lays the groundwork for a fulfilling and harmonious relationship.

The evening comes to a close and it has either been a good night or it hasn't. Hopefully it has. So, you jump in the car to give him or her a lift home, turn the ignition key and your beloved CD of 1950s music begins to play. Do they sing along or do they eject the CD? I actually had someone do the latter and I was not impressed, but kept it to myself. To me, that is not only the height of rudeness but reveals a selfish and bullying attitude. Ditch 'em!!

Assuming you have made it this far and your date appears to be the potential man or woman for you, let's move on to the initial courtship and getting to know each other better.

CHAPTER 4

The Courtship

As I have already said, you've had the first date and you have a reasonable idea of what you are getting yourself into........or do you?

When I was a child, I was quite shy and somewhat of a loner, which probably made me yearn for an idealized life. Looking back, I realize that because I felt lonely, I often rushed into relationships without fully understanding what I was getting into. I'm not dismissing the existence of love at first sight or childhood sweethearts; those who find their soul mate effortlessly are incredibly fortunate. What I am cautioning against is falling into the trap of making hasty decisions. Take a moment to step back and thoroughly evaluate the situation. In essence, 'try before you buy'. This may sound a bit crude, but it's not intended that way.

During your initial date, you both likely shared general information about your likes, dislikes, hobbies, etc. However, the unfortunate reality is that some people may fabricate details to lure you in before revealing their true selves. This is why the courtship period, or the phase of getting to know each other, is crucial for both confirmation and discovery.

When I was dating, I was a soldier, which some might consider a glamorous job. People often make assumptions based on what they think you do or have done. You might be seen as a shining star or something similar. If, like me, you are paraded around as a sort of trophy because of your profession, it's important to heed those warning signs. Consider your income and prospects as well—are you being valued for who you are as a person, or are you being used as a means to a better life or as a stepping stone? You want someone who appreciates you for who you are. In my case, I should have been more cautious and ended those situations quickly, and so should you.

What should you want or need to know about your prospective partner? EVERYTHING!

In previous paragraphs, I touched on the importance of honesty. The getting to know you stage is crucial for assessing this, and it should be tested thoroughly.

If your partner has a history of infidelity and openly admits it, that's a significant red flag. Reflecting on my own experiences, particularly with a woman I'll refer to as 'woman number one', I should have paid closer attention to such signs. She was engaged when we first met, but she left her fiancé for me. Had I known this from the start, I would have avoided the relationship altogether. Ultimately, this decision came back to haunt me when she had an affair and left me for someone else. As the saying goes, some leopards never change their spots.

I also know someone who married a woman despite her having cheated on him eight times while they were dating. Unsurprisingly, their marriage ended in divorce. Engaging with someone who has a pattern of infidelity is a recipe for heartbreak. Such individuals are often never satisfied and are likely driven by selfish desires.

Let's talk about moods. It takes a lot to make me angry, and I'm generally not a moody person. However, have you ever dated someone or worked with a colleague who is perpetually in a bad mood? While it's understandable if someone has occasional bad days due to personal issues, consistently moody people can make life miserable. Reflecting again on woman number one, she revealed her true nature after the first week, becoming snappy, cranky, and moody. She attributed her moods to her menstrual cycle, a claim I can't personally relate to, but none of the other women I've known behaved similarly. Her irritability was more of a constant state rather than a monthly occurrence, making life with her unpleasant. Relationships should be about love, laughter, and sharing, with occasional bumps along the way. Consistently treating your partner poorly is unacceptable, so it's wise to exit such relationships early.

Consider also their political or social views. You might wonder why this matters, but it does. Everyone has their own views, and mine are centred on live and let live, and equal opportunities for all. Woman number one, who now, interestingly, is a minister of religion, turned out to be a blatant racist, a fact that only became apparent after a couple of years when certain phrases slipped out. Given the current climate of global tension and hatred, do you really want to be with someone who harbours such views? I'm grateful she moved on and is no longer a part of my life. My advice is to steer clear of people who exhibit such negative traits.

Ultimately, relationships should enhance your life, not drain your energy. Be vigilant, pay attention to red flags, and prioritize your happiness and well-being.

Consider the "cake monster"—someone who maintains a fit appearance until they secure your interest, then rapidly gains weight. You know the type: they claim to be a fitness enthusiast, but when you invite them for a run, they're winded in 30 seconds and never join you again. If you love food and are comfortable with a larger body, more power to you. But deceiving someone to lure them in and then letting yourself go completely is unfair to your unsuspecting partner. Remember my earlier point about your subconscious list? Body type might be on it. It's also wise to observe the parents and siblings of your potential partner; it might offer valuable insights.

How are your domestic and cleanliness habits? I'm quite tidy and organized, but some people live in perpetual mess. Dirty clothes scattered around, dishes piling up, cupboards and drawers left open—general filth and chaos. Can you picture it? Some people might change, but most won't. This kind of behaviour often stems from selfishness and laziness. Don't let love blind you to these red flags, especially if you know deep down you can't tolerate living in squalor. You'll end up like I did, becoming the chief domestic engineer, handling all the housework.

It's practical, albeit a bit mercenary, to ensure your potential partner is financially sound and not just using you. I learned this the hard way. Despite being good with money, I made the mistake of paying off woman number one's debts. She promised to cut up her credit card but secretly got another one, saying, "I've never had any money, so I'm going to make the most of it." How selfish is that? Being in debt due to circumstances beyond one's control is one thing, but financial irresponsibility is incredibly frustrating. Throughout our relationship, she spent every penny we had, leaving our joint account overdrawn by hundreds each month. Before meeting her, I had never been in debt! This attitude is similar to those who constantly need the latest gadgets, regardless of the cost or necessity. If you're with someone like this, consider ending the relationship now, or you might end up with nothing.

In summary, pay attention to these crucial aspects in a relationship: honesty about lifestyle and habits, cleanliness, and financial responsibility. Being aware of these factors can save you from significant heartache and frustration in the long run.

In essence, my advice is to have a joint bank account if both of you are good with money and are responsible people. However, treat it with respect and fairness, not as your personal money pit. Always check with each other before making significant purchases as a courtesy. Share the finances, but don't take advantage of each other. My wife and I use a credit card for convenience, ensuring we pay off the balance in full each month to avoid interest charges. It's really that simple.

While it's wonderful to share hobbies with your partner and spend quality time together, it's essential to maintain your individual interests. You both had hobbies and interests before meeting each other, and you shouldn't feel pressured to give them up. For example, you might enjoy fishing with friends occasionally, while your partner might be an avid tennis player or fitness enthusiast. Neither of you should be forced to abandon these activities. If your partner pressures you to give up your hobbies, it might be a sign of selfishness that could worsen over time. I love spending time with my wife, but I would never ask her to give up her interests for me. At the same time, it's important to compromise and enjoy each other's company, even if it means occasionally participating in activities that one of you might not prefer.

Some people need their own space, which is perfectly fine. This can mean having a personal hobby or group activity that they attend regularly. However, if your partner's idea of personal space involves avoiding you for extended periods, it's worth reconsidering the relationship. If they don't want you around for a week, it's a red flag.

My second relationship, with a woman I'll call 'woman number two,' was marked by her extreme selfishness. Shortly after we met, she openly admitted to being selfish, but I ignored this warning sign. I even gave up my career to accommodate her lifestyle, a decision I have regretted ever since. The following examples illustrate her selfish behaviour.

Going to the cinema is a popular activity for many couples, and finding a movie you both enjoy should be a matter of compromise. I always believed in attending events with my partner because that's what couples do. However, I experienced situations where I wanted to see a particular movie, but my partner refused to come with me, even though I always went to see her preferred films to spend time with her. This created a lonely feeling of going to the cinema alone or feeling guilty for leaving her at home, even though it was her choice. On two occasions, I was even coerced into taking her friend's young son and a female co-worker to movies because they didn't want to go alone. Don't be an idiot like I was.

Similarly, during my relationship with woman number two, we attended three concerts, all featuring artists *she* liked, but *I* didn't. I went to be with her, yet when performers I enjoyed came to town, she refused to go, and consequently, I missed out. My advice is to avoid selfish people like this.

So, please remember, ensure fairness in your financial arrangements, respect each other's individual interests, and be wary of selfish behaviour. Relationships should be about mutual respect, compromise, and enjoying each other's company, not sacrificing your happiness and interests for someone else's selfish demands.

How about Mister or Miss I don't like your musical tastes? How is that going? Ideally, during an early "ejector date," you caught a glimpse of this potential future—like a certain Mr. Scrooge seeing his Christmases yet to come—and promptly showed that person the door. If you didn't, how are things going now?

In my case, I was told I could only listen to my music if I were securely locked in a space shuttle orbiting the Earth. I was even told that we should only listen to contemporary music so that our children would do the same. Really? What if I don't enjoy all modern music and cherish my own favourites? Forget that! Happiness is door-shaped, so close it on your way out!

Selfishness in a partner can extend to their interactions with family—both theirs and yours. Do they share their family with you and show a genuine interest in getting to know yours? Consider situations involving children from previous relationships. For instance, woman number one not only left me for someone else but also took our two-year-old son. I only reconnected with him a few years ago, after decades of separation.

My second partner had a two-year-old daughter when we met, and she was a spoiled brat. Despite hoping my presence would influence positive change, her behaviour remained challenging. I had photos of my son, including a framed one I used to display proudly. However, my partner didn't want her daughter confused by another child's image in our home, so I gave in to her demands.

When it comes to children and their upbringing, make sure you and your partner are aligned and in full agreement. It's crucial for a harmonious relationship.

Holiday traditions can also reveal a partner's selfishness. Some of us enjoy spending Christmas at home with family, perhaps with visitors dropping by throughout the day. I'm a homebody who values family time but also respects others' traditions. When I met woman number two, we discussed Christmas plans. I mentioned my tradition of visiting my mother briefly to drop off gifts. . I was promptly informed that she *always* goes round to *her* parents for Christmas dinner and that's that, which then alienated me from *my* family.

The experience wasn't even pleasant—her mother and sister were as unpleasant as she was, making for a dreadful occasion. This is why I advise checking out a partner's family before making long-term commitments.

Reflecting on these experiences, it's clear that domestic

abuse can work both ways, affecting both partners. If you find yourself being slowly isolated from your family due to a selfish and overbearing partner, it's time to reconsider the relationship. Your mental well-being is crucial, and you shouldn't compromise it for someone who doesn't value you or your family.

It is essential to ensure that your partner respects your interests and traditions, values family connections, and aligns with you on important matters like finances and child-rearing. If they don't, it's better to end the relationship sooner rather than later to avoid further emotional turmoil.

Another form of selfishness to be wary of is the person who frequently uses the word "my." You know the type: "my car," "my house," "my kid"—as if these things and people don't belong to both of you. Both woman number one and woman number two in my life exhibited this behaviour, and they were the most selfish people I've ever met. If you're encountering this and haven't yet committed to a relationship with such a person, it's time to reconsider. It's your life, so take charge and distance yourself from them.

Hopefully, you haven't fallen into the traps I did and are on your way to a blissful life. However, beware: things can still take a turn for the worse once you move in together, whether as cohabitants or after marriage. It's no surprise that I refer to my ex-partners as woman number one and two. We all know what a number one and two refer to, don't we? If not, look it up and have a laugh at their expense.

Now, let's get to the crucial part. If you're fortunate enough to avoid the issues mentioned, consider your partner's reaction when you either popped the question or discussed a future together. If they were genuinely excited, had a loving expression, and said yes right away, then you've likely found the right person.

But what if they looked stunned in a negative way, couldn't answer, said they needed to think about it, or responded with "perhaps one day"? If they need time to think about it, that's a red flag. You might be in a state of confusion now, but don't waste your life on someone who doesn't love you or want to spend their life with you. It's better to end it now than to live in uncertainty and doubt.

Please be cautious of partners who exhibit selfish behaviours, whether through language, actions, or attitudes towards family and finances. Ensure that you and your partner are aligned on important matters and respect each other's interests and traditions. Most importantly, recognize the signs of a genuine, loving relationship versus one where you're merely tolerated or taken advantage of.

Your happiness and well-being are paramount. Don't settle for less than you deserve. If you recognize any of these red flags in your relationship, it might be time to reconsider your options and prioritize your own life and happiness.

CHAPTER 5

Living Together

Moving in together or getting married is a significant and transformative step in any relationship. It's a time when you truly learn everything about each other—your habits, traits, and little idiosyncrasies that might not have been obvious before. This period can either solidify your bond or reveal deal-breakers that make you reconsider your future together. You may discover that the person you thought was wonderful is, in fact, not the right partner for you.

If you find yourself on the verge of breaking away from a bullying partner, or if some of these warning signs resonate with your current relationship, don't be afraid to make the break. If it means going through a divorce, then so be it. My experience has taught me that if the other person doesn't want you, it's futile to plead or cry over them. They've made their mind up, and nothing you can say, promise, or do will change that.

When my first serious relationship ended, I was blindsided

by woman number one's infidelity. She made it her mission to make me feel like everything was my fault. I was ignored, she spent a lot of time out with her 'friends,' there was no love in our life, and she even went on holiday alone, leaving our bank account overdrawn. After the breakup, I discussed her behaviour with a friend who admitted they had treated their own partner similarly due to guilt from an affair. I was devastated and embarrassed, never imagining this could happen to me.

In hindsight, I regret not taking control of the divorce. I told her that if she wanted it, she should pay for it, and she used the opportunity to spread false stories about me. She even had the audacity to present me with the divorce papers on my birthday. Though it stung at the time, looking back, it was indeed a happy birthday because it marked the beginning of my freedom. I wish I had initiated the divorce; it would have exposed her lies and saved me some embarrassment.

When you're in a toxic relationship, the initial feelings of upset, hurt, and loneliness can be overwhelming. But once you realize that you can wake up each morning and be yourself, it's a profound feeling of freedom and relief. At the time of writing, my wife and I have been together for 19 years, and they have been the happiest years of my life. It *is* possible to find true happiness after leaving a bad relationship.

Have you ever heard the term "happy wife, happy life"? I've heard it many times, and I think its nonsense. This concept can apply to "happy husbands" too, but it oversimplifies the reality of a healthy relationship. Marriage or living together is a two-way street. By this stage, you should be in love, and love is about mutual care, partnership, and making decisions together. It's not about one person controlling the other or ruling the roost. When one partner dominates, it often indicates an abusive relationship where the abuser maintains control, or the other partner becomes so weary of the mistreatment that they simply play along.

A relationship should be a partnership, with both people putting in effort. When I was with woman number two, she worked a part-time job for about 22.5 hours a week, while I worked a full-time job of 58 hours a week plus a part-time job adding another 80 hours per month. I was exhausted. A caring partner would have offered to work more hours so I could cut back. Not this woman. She bluntly said, "I'll never work full time because I like my days off." Even when I expressed my need to quit the part-time job due to exhaustion, her response was, "But the money is good." If you find yourself with someone who doesn't care about your well-being and prioritizes money over your health, it's time to reconsider the relationship. Such a person is not worth your time.

Just be aware that moving in together or getting married reveals the true nature of your relationship. If you encounter signs of selfishness, lack of care, or control, take them seriously. Your happiness and well-being are paramount. Don't settle for a partner who doesn't value you. If you recognize any of these warning signs, consider your options and prioritize your own life and happiness. It's better to be alone and happy than in a relationship that drains you.

Before you moved in together, what was your love life like, and how has it changed now? Was intimacy a daily or weekly occurrence? Who usually initiated it? While the intimate side of a relationship isn't everything, it is undeniably one of the most vital aspects. It's the one thing that only the two of you can share, creating a unique bond.

By now, you may have noticed changes in your intimacy, or perhaps everything remains as it was. If both of you used to initiate lovemaking but now it only happens when your partner wants it, something may be wrong. This shift could indicate that the initiator has taken control of the relationship. Was there an abundance of affection initially that has now dwindled? If so, it's concerning. If you are being cheated on, intimacy might stop altogether—why would they cheat on their new fling with you?

If your relationship is based on you fulfilling a role, such as a parent to their child or a financial provider, the romantic aspect may plummet to the point where it happens rarely, if at all. This can be incredibly frustrating. How is the general affection in your relationship? If you try to hug or kiss them, do they push you away? When you say "I love you," do they respond with warmth, or just a nod?

If any of this resonates with you, it's crucial to have an honest conversation with your partner or take a hard look at your life and ask if this is what you truly want. It's challenging to make a break, but for your sanity, heart, and peace of mind, you may need to do it.

How controlling or thoughtless is your partner? Are they dictating your life? My second partner was incredibly selfish. If she didn't like something of mine, it had to go—either slyly thrown out without my knowledge or consigned to the attic or basement, out of my reach. Have you experienced this?

This happened to me many times. For instance, my record collection suddenly disappeared and ended up in the attic so

I couldn't listen to my music. The most hurtful and thought-less act involved two tailor-made suits that belonged to my late father, which I had kept as a remembrance of him. My partner asked if she could take a rarely worn coat of mine to a charity shop. I agreed, but when I checked my wardrobe a week later, I found several of my suits missing, including my father's suits. I was heartbroken, but she was oblivious. She had picked out items she didn't like and got rid of them. How dare she? Who does that? Obviously, a selfish and thoughtless person who should have been ditched on the spot.

If the shoe had been on the other foot, I wonder how she would have reacted? But then again, a decent person would never do that. If you're in a relationship with someone who exhibits such controlling and thoughtless attitudes, it's time to seriously reconsider the relationship. Ditch the swine and prioritize your well-being. Your happiness and sanity are too important to be compromised by someone who doesn't respect or value you.

How are your social interactions, especially with your partner's family? Do you get along well with them? Are you able to see your own family? In my experience, I rarely saw her family because she didn't like to share her time with them... except on Christmas Day. Most weekends, she would visit her parents alone, and if I asked to join, she would remind me that they were her family, not mine. Consequently, I never really got to know them. Does this sound familiar to you?

As for seeing my own family, that was out of the question because she didn't like them. Being told that you can visit them alone isn't a solution, as it forces you to constantly explain your partner's absence, and there are only so many excuses you can make. How many of us have severed ties with our families because of this situation? It's not fair, is it? If you're in a similar situation, it's a clear sign to reconsider the relationship.

Fortunately, she didn't like going out much, probably because it would involve me or it wasn't somewhere she wanted to go. On the rare occasions we did go out, it never started well because everything had to be according to her preferences, including what I wore. In a loving relationship, you value your partner's opinion and appreciate their feedback on your appearance. However, she would always criticize my clothing choice and pressure me into changing, creating a bad atmosphere before we even left the house.

When it came to choosing events, it was always on her terms. If my friends were attending, she would refuse to engage with them, insisting they come to her. This behaviour eventually led me to avoid work functions altogether. At the few parties we attended with her friends, she would abandon me to socialize with them. One occasion stands out in my memory: I was receiving an important award at work, a proud moment for me. She had no interest in my achievement and immediately asked who else was going. Knowing she disliked my colleagues and their partners, she refused to attend, leaving me to go alone. I had to explain her absence to everyone, and eventually, I just told the truth. If you're experiencing something similar, don't stand for it. Such behaviour won't change because they are too wrapped up in their own self-importance.

Holidays followed the same pattern. We only went where she wanted, and she had no interest in mingling or getting to know fellow travellers. Then there was the issue of communication. With selfish and controlling partners, you lose the ability to decide what words come out of your own mouth. Before going anywhere, I received briefings on what I could and couldn't say, and during events, if I strayed from the script, I would get a painful nudge under the table. Afterwards, I would endure a debriefing full of complaints. It reached a point where I hardly spoke to anyone at functions, leading to more criticism for not talking enough—a no-win situation.

One incident that still irritates me involved my fortieth birthday. A friend asked if I would be having a party, and before I could answer, she interjected with a firm "No!" Her behaviour makes me sick just thinking about it. If any of this resonates with you, it's a sign to seriously reconsider your relationship. You deserve to be with someone who respects you and values your relationships with family and friends. Don't make the same mistakes I did—prioritize your happiness and well-being.

Let's talk about your home and family life. Do you or your partner have a child from a previous relationship? In my situation, my son was taken from me, and my second partner had a young daughter. Ideally, I'd envisioned a "Brady Bunch" scenario, where both families come together seamlessly, with the children referring to their new parents as "Mum" and "Dad," not using terms like "step-parents" or "step-siblings." I believe those terms were coined by someone who didn't want to embrace another person's child fully. Of course, if the biological parent is still involved, that's a different situation.

Nonetheless, you'd hope the new partner loves your child as their own.

Parenting is a critical job, and how you raise your family should be a joint decision. You want your children to grow up to be responsible and kind, with both parents supporting each other in instilling these values. However, it became evident that my second partner wanted me solely to complete her family image—mother, father, child—but not to have any say in her daughter's upbringing. This left me in a difficult position. Simple requests, like asking her daughter to tidy her room, would result in significant conflicts because my partner would undermine me in front of the child. Despite my efforts, her daughter's behaviour deteriorated because she knew my words held no weight. This dynamic negatively impacted our entire family life. If this sounds familiar, it might be time to reconsider your relationship.

Before my second partner and I got married, we had a son together. You might wonder why we had a child if our relationship wasn't great. At the time, I believed that having a child might be the key to a happy life, which it was, briefly. My son became the apple of my eye, and I was determined that he wouldn't turn out like his sister. I hoped that his positive behaviour might even influence her.

However, the problems began because we weren't married. My partner insisted that our son would have her last name because, according to the law, I had no parental rights. She revelled in reminding me that since we weren't married, I had no legal responsibilities or rights as a father. Who says that, let alone follows through with it?

Ultimately, being in a relationship where you're not

respected or valued is detrimental to your mental and emotional health. If you're dealing with a partner who doesn't support or appreciate you, it's essential to evaluate your situation critically. You deserve a partner who respects your role in the family and works with you as a team. If you're experiencing these issues, don't hesitate to plan your escape and seek a happier, healthier life.

Looking back now, it's painfully clear to me that I was enduring bullying and psychological abuse in my relationship. What infuriates me the most is how she manipulated me into being someone I wasn't. Whenever she embarrassed me in front of our children, my reaction was to storm off and vent loudly in private. I felt completely out of control, seeking solace alone. Ranting was the extent of my outbursts, except for moments when I'd sit on the floor sobbing uncontrollably. Even then, I was told to stop crying, disregarding my feelings and emotional turmoil. If I craved sympathy, I might as well have searched for it between "shit" and "syphilis" in the dictionary! Looking back, I should have ended things with her, and if you're in a similar situation, perhaps you should too.

Not only did she exhibit this disgraceful behaviour, but I was also taken for granted? Some partners love to believe they're exceptional parents, but when it comes to supporting and participating in their children's lives, their commitment wanes. How many of you find yourselves doing the school drop-offs, attending swimming lessons, or coaching football purely out of love? That was me. Working shifts meant I wasn't always home, so inevitably, these responsibilities fell to me on my days off. I didn't mind; in fact, I loved it. However, Miss Lazy Pants assumed it was my duty because she worked "long hours". She believed she deserved a rest, leaving me to handle these tasks alone. The silver lining was that these moments allowed me to bond with our kids without interference.

The same went for fun activities like taking the kids to see Disney or Pixar films. She had no interest and readily passed that duty to me as well. Who wouldn't want to enjoy such moments with their children, especially someone like her, who worked in childcare? It was baffling. Nonetheless, I cherished these experiences and cherished watching the films myself. So here's my advice: if you're in a toxic relationship and your partner shows little interest in family activities, it's time to seriously evaluate whether their negativity is worth enduring. Deep down, you probably know that everyone, including your children, would be better off without that person's influence.

Do you like family secrets? I certainly don't. As our son and daughter grew older, I felt it was time to discuss my firstborn, but once again, I was shut down. My attempts to acknowledge my past, including keeping a photo of my first-born, were dismissed. At this point, the relationship between my wife, daughter, and myself was at its lowest. I faced mockery from both of them openly, even witnessing them reject gifts I gave them. It felt like a competition to see who could hurt me more. To top it off, I later discovered that despite her assurances, my wife had informed our son about his long-lost brother—something I believed was my responsibility alone. It was a spiteful betrayal.

After enduring these and other indignities, I finally decided to end the marriage. I never anticipated being divorced once, let alone twice. But to anyone feeling stigmatized by divorce, I say this: don't worry. Your life and happiness are paramount. Have faith, take the leap, and you won't regret prioritizing your well-being.

CHAPTER 6

The Break Up

When you find yourself facing a breakup, there's more to it than simply starting over. My advice? Start by arming yourself with knowledge. It's crucial to understand your rights. If legal advice seems out of reach financially, turn to resources like your local Citizens Advice Bureau where you can get free legal guidance. In many countries, divorce applications can be obtained directly from the court at no cost. Keep that option in mind.

Consider the nature of your breakup. Will it be amicable, or are you dealing with ongoing abuse? This distinction is pivotal because it will shape how you plan your exit strategy. Perhaps you need to make a clean break, quietly and discreetly, ensuring your safety and peace of mind by leaving when your partner is absent.

Reflecting on my experiences, I've had two very different breakups. With my first partner, there was no preparation or coordination; she disappeared overnight with our son and all our belongings. I had no idea where she went and only communicated with her through her lawyer, adding to the distress.

The second breakup, however, saw me finally taking charge, which was empowering. But even then, I had to meticulously plan my departure. It was late October when I decided to leave, but I told her I would wait until after Christmas, not wanting to ruin the holiday for the children. Yet, even in this moment, she managed to assert control. I made the mistake of giving her everything in the divorce settlement out of concern for my children's stability—home, possessions, everything. She wasted no time asserting her dominance by demanding I leave before Christmas, showing no remorse or sadness after 15 years together. She got exactly what she wanted: everything.

Learn from my experience: don't make my mistakes. You've worked hard for what you own, and you're entitled to your fair share. Don't let guilt sway you. Claim what is rightfully yours.

Do you know what though? I *did* get the last laugh in one respect. Can you believe that this woman thought that after all she had put me through over the years that she would be my coffee buddy? Yep, she told me we could be friends and meet up for coffee after the split. She probably had it in mind to carry on with the controlling behaviour. Well I not only put her straight, but also put her nose out of joint, so to speak. I told her a few home truths and said "Do you really think that after treating me like shit all these years that I want to be your friend? The only time I'll be seeing you is when I collect and drop my son off at your front door. End of story!"

I cannot tell you how good I felt. The last laugh was had by me!

So, if you're navigating a breakup, educate yourself, plan carefully, and assert your rights. Don't repeat my errors; prioritize your well-being and secure your future.

CHAPTER 7

Let the Good
Life Begin

Now, there are a couple of concepts I've already touched upon: "falling in love with love itself" and "finding someone who loves me for who I am, not for who they want me to become." These ideas are pivotal in many lives, as is the challenge of dealing with partners who try to assert dominance over the relationship, believing their approval is necessary for every decision you make.

For me, not having experienced reciprocal love before, I think I fell in love with the idea of love itself. Feeling lonely and yearning for love, it's natural to be flattered when someone shows interest in you romantically. It can be a relief to believe that loneliness won't be a permanent state. The initial excitement and the fluttering feeling in your stomach can be quite intoxicating. However, from my own experiences, I advise enjoying these moments while also maintaining a level-headed perspective. Don't rush to declare undying love after the first date. Instead, take the time to observe the person's characteristics, attitudes, and overall behaviour. Reflecting on past experiences might reveal warning signs that could indicate this person isn't right for you. Stay calm and protect yourself emotionally.

Desiring to be loved for who you genuinely are is a universal longing. Therefore, don't settle for someone who clearly wants to mold you into something you're not. It's important to differentiate between recognizing your own flaws and actively seeking personal growth versus being controlled by someone who wants to dictate your every move. Don't enter into relationships with control freaks; heed the warning signs I've explained previously.

Whether you're new to dating or re-entering the dating scene, remember that your life is unfolding anew. There truly is someone out there for everyone. If you desire a partner, take proactive steps to find them. They could be in unexpected places like a bar, at work, or through online platforms.

Depending on your age and circumstances, you might find online dating to be a viable option. I personally tried reputable dating websites rather than casual swipe-based apps, and that's where I met my wife. The beauty of dating sites lies in the control they afford you. You can choose not to meet anyone unless you decide its right, and even then, you select the venue, ensuring your comfort and safety. It's crucial to craft a profile that's completely honest about who you are and what you seek in a partner. I made it clear in my introduction that I was looking for someone who accepts me as I am, not someone intent on changing me. This served as a filter, deterring selfish individuals who sought to control.

Fortunately, I was contacted soon after by my beautiful wife. When we met, we instantly connected and fell deeply in love. We discovered each other on our own terms, which felt authentic and right. Despite the hardships I've faced, if they led me to my wonderful wife, then they were worth enduring. I've never felt as loved, appreciated, and genuinely wanted as I do now.

I hope this book has guided you effectively, highlighting the pitfalls to watch for in others' characters, identifying qualities of a good partner, and warning signs of a bad one.

Good luck on your journey. May you find true love and eternal happiness in your life.

The Beginning.........

About the Author

Jack Mallory has not only worked in the field of coaching and personal development mentoring, but also draws upon his years of life experience in his desire to help others learn from their own mistakes, and those of others, in order that may have what we all desire; a happy and fulfilling life.